My details

Name: ______________________

School: ______________________

Friends: ______________________

Interests: ______________________

____

____

____

Before you begin writing ...

Here are the 3Ps that will help you with your writing: posture, pencil grip and paper position. You will be reminded about these as you go through the book.

Posture

1. Sit up straight at your table.
2. Put your feet flat on the floor.
3. Keep your wrist straight and resting on the table.

Pencil or pen grip

1. Rest the pencil or pen on your middle finger.
2. Pinch your index finger and thumb together gently.

Left-handed

Right-handed

Paper

1. The paper is on an angle and held steady by your non-writing hand.
2. For right-handers, the page will tilt to the left.
3. For left-handers, the page will tilt to the right.

Left-handed

Right-handed

OXFORD UNIVERSITY PRESS

Revision

Print and cursive

Before you begin, complete the checklist below.

- ❑ I have my feet flat on the floor.
- ❑ My back is up nice and straight.
- ❑ I can hold the pencil or pen correctly.

Consolidate your printing of lower-case letters.

a b c d e f g h i j k l m n o p q r s t u v w x y z

Consolidate your printing of capital letters.

A B C D E F G H I J K L M

N O P Q R S T U V W X Y Z

Consolidate your numerals and punctuation marks.

1 2 3 4 5 6 7 8 9 10 15 20 . , “ ” ’ ? ! ; :

Finish the table below. The first one is done for you.

55 489	Fifty-five thousand, four hundred and eighty-nine
5632	
15 311	
5 110 000	
506 210	
50 766	

Copy the sentences below:

Participating in regular physical activity is good for your health. It is important to find activities that you enjoy. This can include playing a sport or running.

Copy these words

bike riding

skateboarding

jogging

stretching

physical

gardening

Speed loops

Learning intention: To practise our speed loops to and from f

Speed loops to and from f

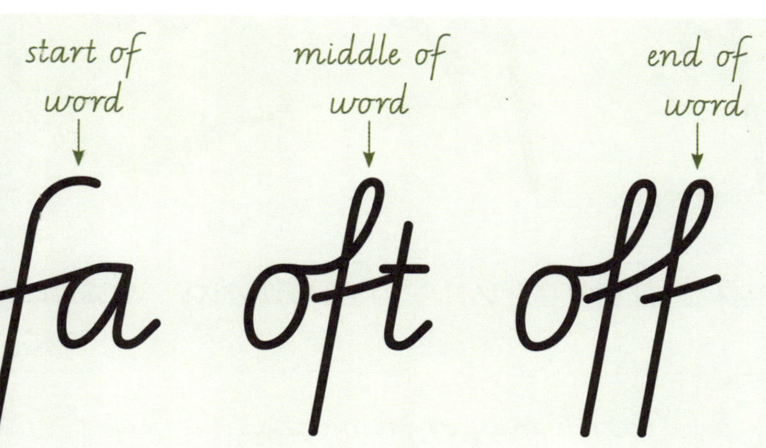

Speed loops are fluid movements used to create loops and curves in the letters of a word. Speed loops make joining letters quicker.

We've learnt about the looped f. Let's start practising speed loops with the letter f.

fi

join from the crossbar

Practise writing the letter f at the beginning of a word.

fa fa fr fr fe fe fi fi fl fl fo fo

field fairness fantastic futsal frisbee

speed loop to f

ifu

join from the crossbar

Practise writing f to and from other letters.

oft oft aft aft ife ife ifu ifu afy afy

leafy beautiful life after before referee often

if

Practise writing when f is the last letter of a word.

ef ef urf urf iff iff uff uff rf rf af af

surf bluff puff self proof chief turf

Learning intention: To practise joins from the letter f at the start of a word

I am successful when I can:
- ❑ sit with my back straight
- ❑ hold the pencil or pen correctly
- ❑ position my paper
- ❑ make my joins from f sloped.

When joining from f, the join is sloped.

fi fr

fr fu fi fr fu from funny friendship finishing fitness

Fine motor skills task: Draw a picture of you and your family or friends having fun.

Family fun with games and sports is a wonderful way to promote physical activity among family members. Some ideas for family-friendly games and sports include playing hide and seek, swimming and hiking. A fun indoor activity is to create an obstacle course for your fit and fearless family members to complete.

Self-assessment Draw a star next to your best writing. Think about size, slope and how well you completed your joins.

Remember, to make a join to f, loop the f at the top, lift your pen and use the crossbar to join to the next letter.

Practise by tracing the letters and then copying them.

ef ef ______ uf uf ______

af af ______ if if ______

surfing often brief mischief careful roof leaf softball

Copy the picture of the surfer in the box provided.

Speed loops from g, j, y and z

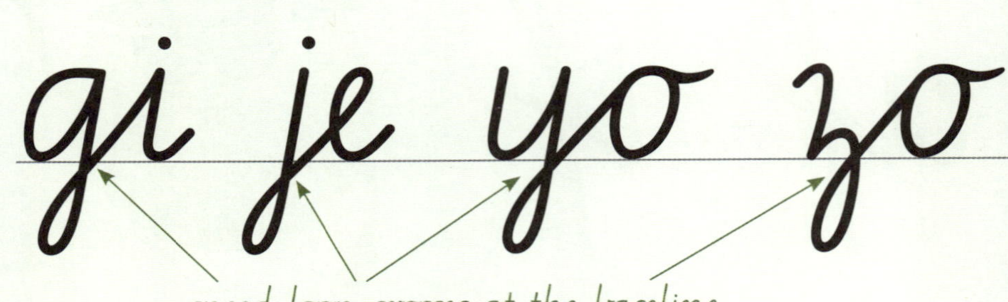

Learning intention:
To use speed loops to increase fluency and speed when writing

Speed loops make joining letters faster and neater. They help with fluency because there are fewer times that you lift your pencil from the page.

Practise these speed loops from g.

ga ge gi gl go gr gu ga ge gi gl go gr

golf gymnastics goalkeeper game grip goalie grade

Practise these speed loops from j.

ja ju ji jo ja ju jumping joggers join just adjust subject

Practise these speed loops from y.

ya ye yi yo yu yl yr ya ye yi yo yu yl yr

yachting yoga yellow young yearly yaw yard

Practise these speed loops from z.

z z z zoo zap zip buzz fuzzy jazz fizz

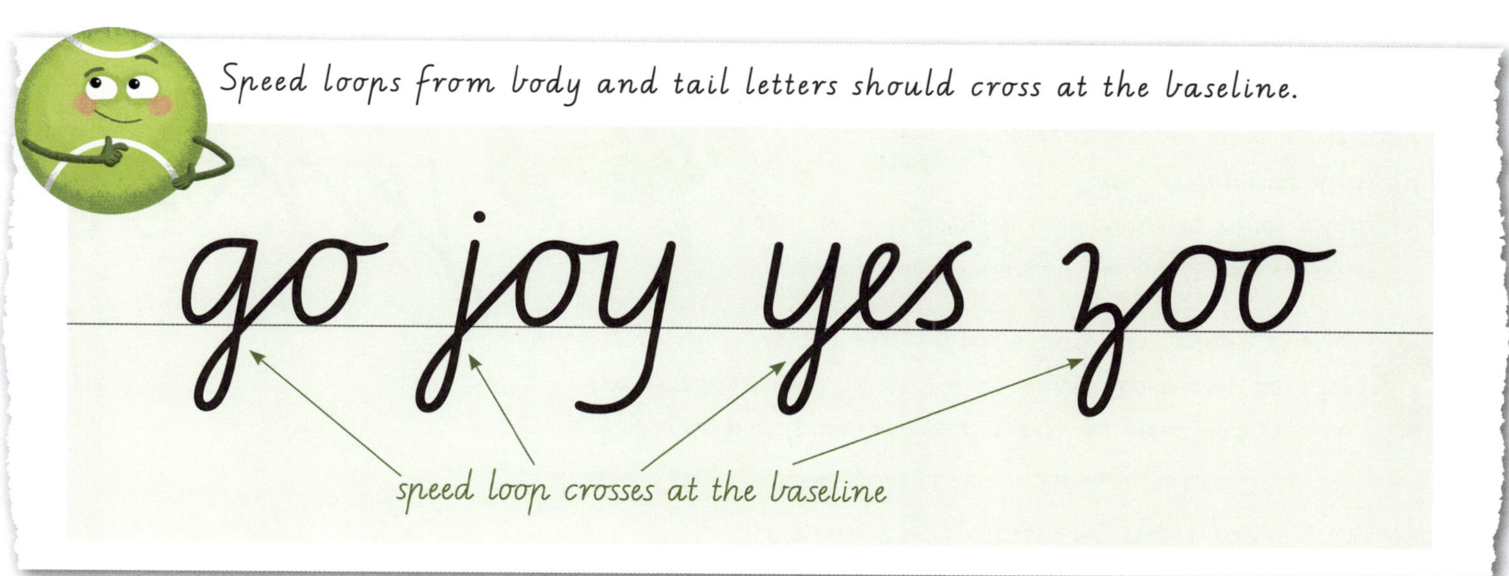

Practise your speed loops by copying these words, which are commonly misspelt.

jewellery		judgement	
challenge		congratulate	
rhythm		hygiene	

Practise your speed loops by copying these sentences.

The sport of gymnastics is challenging, with athletes needing a combination of strength, agility, flexibility and coordination.

Gymnastics dates back thousands of years, with roots in Ancient Greece, where it formed part of the physical training for soldiers.

I am successful when I can:

- ❑ sit with my back straight
- ❑ hold the pencil or pen correctly
- ❑ position my paper
- ❑ use speed loops to increase my fluency and speed.

Speed loops are not used if the letter is at the end of the word. We don't need one because we are at the end of the word, so no speed is needed.

Practise your speed loops by copying this passage.

The "yellow jersey" is a term used in cycling, particularly in one of the most famous races: the Tour de France. The Tour de France is typically held annually in July. It consists of multiple stages, which can include flat stages, mountain stages, time trials and more. The rider who wears the yellow jersey at the end of each stage is recognised as the race leader. Wearing the yellow jersey is a significant honour in the sport of cycling and often indicates that the rider is a strong contender for winning the overall race.

Self-assessment

Draw a star next to your best writing. Think about size, slope and how well you completed your speed loops.

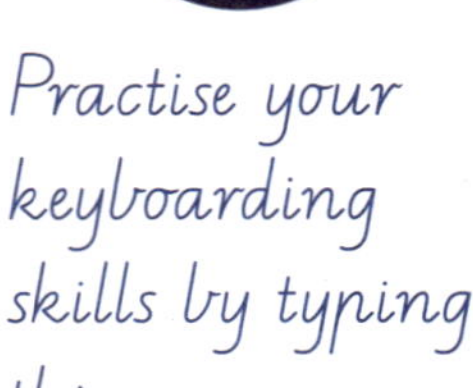

Practise your keyboarding skills by typing this passage.

Copy this passage with cursive handwriting and speed loops.

Australia has a rich history of producing sporting champions who have achieved amazing success. A few notable Australian sporting heroes include Sir Donald Bradman, Dawn Fraser, Rod Laver, Raelene Boyle, Evonne Goolagong Cawley, Shane Gould, Shane Warne, Cathy Freeman, Ian Thorpe and Dylan Alcott. These people made a significant contribution to their sport; many of them also actively engage in their communities through sporting and community initiatives and projects.

Draw a picture of an Australian sporting hero.

Self-assessment

Draw a star next to your best writing. Think about size, slope and how well you completed your speed loops.

Practise your keyboarding skills by typing this passage.

Speed loops to b, h, k and l

Learning intention:
To use speed loops to increase fluency and speed when writing

speed loop crosses at the top body line

lb th

I am successful when I can:
- ❏ use speed loops from body and tail letters
- ❏ cross speed loops across the top body line.

Tip! The letters b, k, h and l do not need a speed loop when they appear at the start of a word.

Practise these speed loops to b, h, k and l on this page and the next.

b b b b ab be ib ob ub bb lb rb bl

able table football volleyball tribe able bulb robe

h h h h oh gh ph sh th ch ah oh gh

triathlon shine think thigh marathon workout archery

To enhance their agility and strength, football players often work out at the gym. Becoming a football player requires skill, hard work and confidence. Football players work hard to improve their ball handling and kicking skills.

Try not to make your speed loops too big or they will slow down your writing.

l l l l il gl ll lm ln ol pl rl sl tl

golf cycling wrestling athletics goalie walk happily volley

k k k k ak ek ck ok lk nk rk sk uk

walk risk work rink kick jacket kayak strike kit

Copy this sentence, focusing on your speed loops.

Soccer, also known as football in many parts of the world, involves a wide range of skills that players need to learn in order to excel. Players need to kick the ball towards the goal and to move swiftly across the field by passing, dribbling and controlling the ball.

Peer feedback

Ask a partner to review your work and provide feedback.

Two stars (two things you did well)

One wish (one suggestion on something you can improve)

I am successful when I can:

- ❑ sit with my back straight
- ❑ hold the pencil or pen correctly
- ❑ position my paper
- ❑ cross speed loops at the body line.

loops cross at the body line

ph ck

Remember, speed loops to ascenders cross at the body line.

Copy these words with speed loops that cross at the body line.

martial wrestling bowling racquetball kiteboarding

hiking snowboarding football hurdles archery

Remember, the loop is only used when joining to these letters, not if the word ends with these letters.

✓ jumping NOT jumping ✗

no loop

Practise your speed loops by copying these words.

bowling		strike	
hockey		pucks	
physical		walking	
kayaking		paddling	
basketball		goal	
handball		volleyball	

Practising joins

Diagonal joins

Learning intention:
To revise diagonal joins when forming letters

Remember, a diagonal join is made from the bottom of one letter to the top of the next letter.

Diagonal joins occur when one letter smoothly transitions to another at an angle. Try not to lift your pencil or pen.

Move along the path without going over the edges.

Practise these diagonal joins.

am an ap ar at py ce cr di dr dy he hs

in is le li mp mi ni ex te ti un uc ix

Trace over these letter combinations and then copy them on the lines below. Remember not to lift your pencil or pen.

ni ni ni eu eu eu ne ne ne

ep ep ep mi mi mi nu nu nu

di di di ip ip ip li li li

Use diagonal joins to practise these sentences.

An active lifestyle includes regular physical activity and healthy eating. This means making an effort to be active through the day.

Word building!

heal

Meaning: to cure or save; make whole, sound and well (from Old English)

Using the base word "heal", how many words can you form?

For example: heal + th = health

Don't forget: we often change the y at the end of a word to an i before adding the suffix.

Prefix	Base word	Suffixes			List your words here
un-	heal	-s -ing -ed -er			
		-th	-y	-er -est -ly -ness	

Diagonal joins to tall letters

Learning intention: To practise our diagonal joins

I am successful when I can:
- ❑ sit with my back straight
- ❑ hold the pencil or pen correctly
- ❑ position my paper
- ❑ make diagonal joins smoothly.

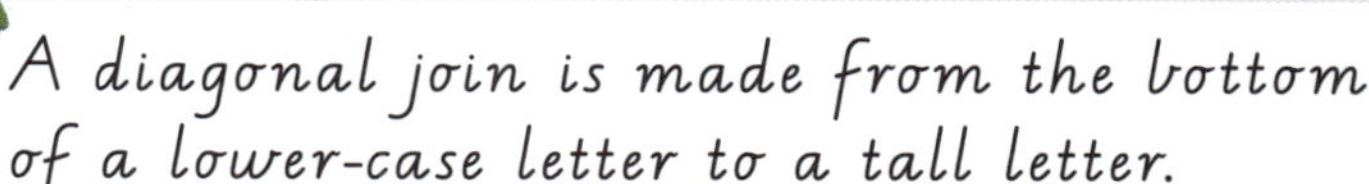

A diagonal join is made from the bottom of a lower-case letter to a tall letter.

Use a sweeping movement to practise writing these diagonal joins to tall letters.

al th et ub d ch nk it el ul lt lk at

Tip! The top of the letter t stretches up to half the height of tall letters like l, d or b. The crossbar on t needs to be level with the top of the letter body.

activities ______

fitness ______

nutrient ______

active ______

stretch ______

Practise these diagonal joins to tall letters.

Playing a sport is a fantastic way of keeping fit and healthy.

There are a variety of sports and activities to engage in.

Enjoying regular physical activity has many health benefits.

Word building!

Add the suffix -ing to the words below.

Remember to drop the e before adding -ing.

If the last letter is a consonant and comes after a vowel, double the consonant before adding -ing.

swim		hurdle	
ride		wrestle	
drop		bike	
bounce		run	
skate		cycle	
dance		hop	
jog		jump	

Fine motor skills task: Help Ava through the maze to find her ball. Be careful not to touch the edges or lift your pencil or pen.

Drop-in joins

Learning intention:
To revise drop-in joins

Extend exit, lift and drop in the next letter.

When we do a diagonal join to an anti-clockwise letter, the exit from the first letter reaches high towards the top of the next letter. We then drop the next letter in place. Drop-in joins avoid retracing and contribute to the legibility and elegance of cursive handwriting.

The letters a, c, d, g, o and q are dropped into place. Write these drop-in joins.
The dot shows you when to lift the pencil or pen.

ac ca dg eq ma da ac ca dg ma ac na ma

ic ud aq ug id eg ec nd iq da ig ed uc ag

Practise these drop-in joins.

fantastic sweat exercise start agility light edge

sport posture balance powerful conditioning stretch

muscles body workout training practise athletic

Self-assessment Underline your smoothest join. Circle a join that needs more practice.

Copy the sentences below, practising your drop-ins and holding your pencil or pen correctly.

Active games and family activities are other fun ways to lead an active lifestyle. Games such as hide and seek, capture the flag, tag and hopscotch are all fun and engaging activities. There are lots of things to do outside in the fresh air. Try bike riding, going for a bush walk or playing a game in the park. The whole family can enjoy being active together. Make it fun and do it often to feel the benefits.

Fine motor skills task: *Follow the steps to draw the picture.*

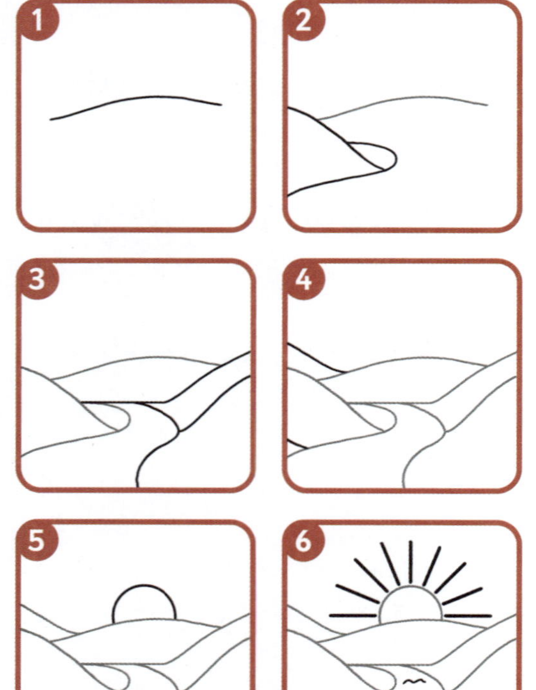

Horizontal joins

small dip
retrace
retrace

or ra ok

Learning intention:
To use horizontal joins for b, o, r, v and w

Horizontal joins are made from letters that finish near the top.

Practise these horizontal joins.

oi om on op or ot ou ov ow ox rb ri rm

rn ru rv rw va vi vo wi wa wn wo

outings boost workout development explore crucial

Word building!

Build three or more words from the base words, choosing the right suffixes from below. The first one is done for you.
-ment, -ed, -ing, -able, -y, -ive, -ion

Don't forget: we usually drop the e at the end of words when adding a suffix.

discover	discovered	discovering	discovery
participate			
engage			
interact			
cooperate			
coordinate			
enjoy			

Learning intention: To practise horizontal and diagonal joins to s

Joins to s

I am successful when I can:
- ❑ sit with my back straight
- ❑ hold the pencil or pen correctly
- ❑ position my paper
- ❑ choose the regular s for horizontal joins, and the short s for diagonal joins
- ❑ join across to the top of the s and then retrace.

Horizontal joins to s

retrace

us

Diagonal joins to s

is

modified s

When joining horizontally to s, write the regular s. When joining diagonally, write the short s.

Practise these joins to s.

os rs fs ws us is as ts ls ns us es

lost toss history activities emphasis composes occurs

On the lines below, practise joining the s with a diagonal join, making the top of the s shorter.

Australian sport has a rich and diverse history, with a strong emphasis on outdoor activities and both traditional and modern sports. Among the most popular sports are tennis, cricket, netball, soccer and Australian rules football.

Copy these words with joins to s onto the lines below. Underline the words that use a horizontal join to s.

news best muscle stress socks household stamina most

speed skating members drawstring positive sustain offside

Copy these words with joins to s onto the lines below. Circle the words that use diagonal joins to s.

skates first rackets students skills

matches games blossom memories fastest

Which letters always come before a horizontal join to s?

Rewrite these words, adding all possible joins.

because

most

emphasis

activities

Joke time!
What is an insect's favourite sport?
Cricket!

Fine motor skills task: *Practise your drawing skills by following these examples to build a picture.*

1

2

3

4

5

6

Joins to double s

Learning intention: To develop fluency when writing double s

I am successful when I can:
- ❑ sit with my back straight
- ❑ hold the pencil or pen correctly
- ❑ position my paper
- ❑ make my double s clear.

horizontal join to s

gloss glass

diagonal join to s

Copy the words below to practise writing double s.

pass bossy motocross passing toss success lacrosse miss

tossing crossbar dismissal loss wilderness stress breathless

In the game of cricket, a dismissal is when a batter gets out.

There are a few ways a batter can be dismissed. Common forms of dismissal include being caught, bowled or run out. The outcome of the game may hinge on the toss of the coin, because conditions that one side faces now compared to conditions the other side faces later on can dictate the success or struggles for each team throughout the match.

Joins to b, o, r, v and w

Learning intention: To practise joins to b, o, r, v and w

Horizontal joins are made from letters that finish near the top. Remember to add a small dip.

Practise these horizontal joins.

or ra oy re oo rt wi od ol or on os vi

ri wn rr ro om ot wd og ov vi rt we ow

There are many other sports that Australians enjoy, such as basketball, swimming, golf, surfing, cycling and more. Sport plays an important role in Australian culture, by providing entertainment and promoting physical fitness and community engagement.

In cursive handwriting, complete each sentence below, adding the correct punctuation mark at the end of each sentence.

My favourite sport is ____________ because ____________

At school we play ____________

Joins to e

bigger dip

oe re

Learning intention: To practise horizontal joins to e

I am successful when I can:

- ❑ sit with my back straight
- ❑ hold the pencil or pen correctly
- ❑ position my paper
- ❑ make my joins to e connect horizontally, creating a smooth line.

When joining horizontally to e, some letters have a bigger dip than a normal horizontal join. This makes it easier to join.

Practise these horizontal joins to e.

re ve we oe re ve we oe

are have give fervent persevere unwavering relaxed

Participating in sport can have a powerful impact on children, as it can give them the chance to develop physical capabilities and teamwork skills, and learn the value of dedication and hard work. Children who are fervent and passionate about their sport persevere through challenges, have unwavering commitment and strive for excellence.

Word	Part of speech	Meaning	Image
persevere	verb	To keep trying and not give up, even though it is difficult.	
fervent	adjective	To have strong feelings about something and be very sincere and enthusiastic about it.	
strive	verb	To make a great effort to do or achieve something.	

Answer these questions using cursive handwriting.

How do you persevere with a difficult task?

What are you fervent about?

What are you striving to achieve?

Self-assessment

Think about your work in relation to the success criteria.
What did you notice you were able to do well?
What do you need to work on next?

Consolidating

Diagonal — in

Drop-in — Extend exit, lift and drop-in the next letter. — ia

Horizontal — small dip — or

Brush up on your joins!

Copy the letters below and add the diagonal joins.

ai as an cu in es hi ke ur me

Add joins to these letters. Then underline the drop-in joins and circle the diagonal joins.

ar de ce le ag th ca me ea ua do

Write this sentence adding in joins, including drop-in joins.

Engaging in sport provides quality opportunities for recreation and leisure.

Add the joins.

It also provides a source of leisure and a break from daily routines.

Copy this sentence to practise joining to the letter s.

It is essential to use the correct safety equipment for some sports.

Assessment: Practising joins

Rewrite these words in cursive, adding in joins.

fitness		boost	
because		often	
benefits		promote	
careful		balance	
members		active	
workout		health	
explore		physical	
theme		found	
tennis		soccer	

Copy the passage below to practise your joins.

Sports offer numerous benefits, such as improved fitness and fun.

Many different types of leisure activities, including walking,

hiking and playing games, also help to promote wellbeing

and healthy lifestyle habits.

Teacher feedback

Practise your keyboarding skills by typing this passage.

Fluency joins and speed loops

Practising fluency joins

Learning intention:
To practise fluency in joining letters

Practise your fluency joins by copying this text.

Badminton

Badminton is a racket sport played by two or more players. Players use lightweight rackets to strike a shuttlecock. Badminton is played at various skill levels, from backyard games to highly competitive international tournaments.

Softball

Softball is a team sport usually played on a field. It requires a combination of skills, such as batting, throwing, catching and base running. Softball provides great opportunities to develop skills, learn about teamwork and engage in friendly competition.

Netball

Netball is a popular sport incorporating skills such as passing and shooting. Players must work together to pass and catch the ball while trying to outmanoeuvre the other team. The game is played in schools, leagues and at the international level.

Soccer

Soccer is one of Australia's most popular sports. It has a long and rich history in many countries around the world and is sometimes referred to as the "world game". In this fast-paced game, players require skilful footwork, agility and endurance.

More practice for joins with double s

Practise these pairs. Remember that a horizontal join to s uses a regular s. A diagonal join to s uses a modified s. So, for horizontal joins with a double s, you will have two different shaped letter ss next to each other.

oss ess iss uss oss ess iss uss

Practise using cursive handwriting by copying these commonly confused words and their definitions.

lesson – a fixed time when people are taught about a subject or how to do something

lessen – to become or make something become smaller, weaker or less important

Fine motor skills task: Follow the steps and complete the drawing.

Building fluency

Apple and bran muffins

Practise your speed loops by copying these ingredients.

Ingredients

- 2 cups self-raising flour, sifted
- ½ teaspoon baking powder, sifted
- 1 cup wheat bran
- 2 tablespoons brown sugar
- 1 teaspoon ground cinnamon
- 1 large pink lady apple, grated
- 1 cup skim milk
- 2 eggs, lightly beaten
- 2 tablespoons vegetable oil
- ½ cup apple sauce

Practise your keyboarding skills by typing this recipe procedure.

Place flour, baking powder, bran, sugar, cinnamon and apple in a large bowl. Stir to combine. Make a well in the centre. Place milk, eggs, oil and apple sauce into a jug and whisk until just combined. Pour mixture into well and stir gently. Scoop the batter into the muffin tin. Bake for 15 minutes at 170 degrees Celsius. You will be able to smell when they are cooked.

Consolidating

Copy this passage.

Australian rules football is a fast-paced and physical game involving players advancing the ball by either kicking it or handpassing it. The objective of the game is to score the most points. Each goal is worth six points, and each behind is worth one point. A behind is when the ball goes through the behind posts, which are placed on either side of the goal posts. Before Australian rules football, there was the First Nations sport known as marngrook. This game involved kicking and catching a ball made from possum or kangaroo skin.

Copy these sentences to practise your speed loops and fluency joins.

Dylan Alcott is an Australian wheelchair tennis player and disability advocate. He is known for his remarkable achievements in wheelchair tennis and his efforts to promote inclusivity and equality for people with disabilities.

Cathy Freeman is a track and field athlete who is celebrated as one of Australia's greatest sporting heroes. She won gold and lit the Olympic flame at the Sydney Olympics. Freeman's athletic skill and unwavering determination have earned her a special place in Australian hearts.

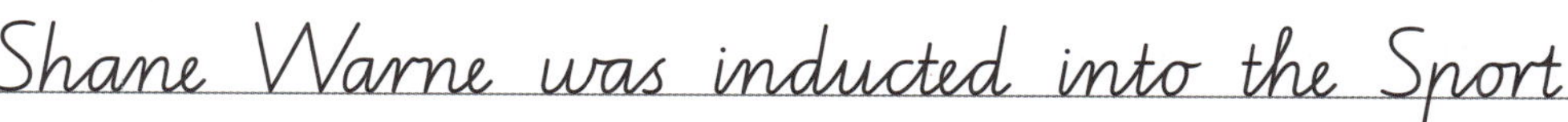

Shane Warne was inducted into the Sport Australia Hall of Fame in 2009 for his contribution to cricket. He transformed the art of leg spin, a type of spin bowling in cricket. Warne's impact on cricket was immense and he remains a cricketing legend in Australia.

Assessment: Fluency joins and speed loops

Copy these words to practise your fluency joins.

spectators brave premier strong showcase pitch

bases penalty strike pass sailing blindside

Copy this passage to practise your fluency joins.

People love to not only participate in sport but also to be spectators. Spectators love watching and cheering on their favourite teams and sportspeople in a variety of sports, including swimming, sailing, motocross, tennis, volleyball and football. Watching sports with other spectators is exciting and fun. Perhaps more importantly, it can also provide a sense of belonging and camaraderie.

Self-assessment

Draw a star next to your best writing. Think about size, slope and how well you completed your fluency joins.

OXFORD UNIVERSITY PRESS

Remember not to make your speed loops too big or they will slow you down.

Practise your speed loops by copying the passage below.

The word "football" can have different meanings depending on the region you live in. It is a term used to describe a variety of different types of sports involved in kicking a ball to score goals. Around the world, the word "football" is associated with what Australians call soccer. In the United States of America, "football" means a different type of sport called gridiron. The field is divided into sections by yard lines, and the game is played with a combination of passing, running and kicking, with the primary focus being to get the ball into the opponent's end zone to score touchdowns.

Peer feedback

Ask a partner to review your work and provide feedback.

Two stars (two things you did well)

One wish (one suggestion on something you can improve)

Rewrite the words below, adding speed loops to the letters that need them.

triumph legend challenge achievement recognition symbol

celebrate skilful jogging potential excellence heritage

Practise your cursive handwriting with speed loops by copying this information about Sir Donald Bradman.

Sir Donald Bradman was inducted into the Sport Australia Hall of Fame in 1985. On that occasion, he said that if anyone deserves a statue, they should be someone who has lived their life with dignity, integrity, courage and modesty. These qualities are in addition to their skill, and are compatible with pride, ambition and competitiveness.

Teacher feedback

Practise your keyboarding skills by typing this passage.

Spacing, size and slope revision

Spacing

Learning intention:
To practise spacing letters and words correctly

It is important to keep your spacing even between letters and words. This will help to make your writing more legible.

sporting champions

Copy the text below focusing on the fluency joins and speed loops. Remember that tall letters and capitals are the same height. Numerals are the same height as short letters.

Some types of motorsports include the 1000 km touring car race

Bathurst 1000 and the Australian Grand Prix, an annual

motor racing event. Drivers have to be very fit to cope with the

force on the car and their bodies as they drive at such fast speeds.

These sporting events provide exciting and thrilling experiences

for both participants and spectators.

Fine motor skills task: Copy the drawing.

Size

Learning intention:

To practise sizing letters correctly and keeping letters between the lines

Focus on keeping your letter size between the lines, as it helps to make your writing easier to read.

I am successful when I can:

- ❏ sit with my back straight
- ❏ hold the pencil or pen correctly
- ❏ position my paper
- ❏ make my letters even in size and keep them between the lines.

Practise your cursive handwriting.

Tennis is not only a competitive sport but also a popular recreational activity and a fun way to stay physically active. The Australian Open is a Grand Slam tournament held annually in Melbourne. Wheelchair tennis follows the same rules as traditional tennis but with a few changes to assist players using wheelchairs. It promotes inclusivity, giving individuals with mobility impairments an opportunity to participate in an active and competitive sport.

Slope

Learning intention: To practise sloping letters correctly, using a slope grid

Use the slope grids below to help you maintain a consistent slope. Copy these words, or write your own words.

recreation

improvement

technique

perseverance

strength

flexibility

Fine motor skills task:
Using these images, create a drawing that reminds you of being active, relaxing or doing something you really enjoy in the outdoors.

Practising correct spacing, size and slope

Practise keeping your letters on the lines. Make sure you keep the size consistent.

good example	example of what to avoid
Being active is fun	Being active is fun

What is wrong with the appearance of these words? Can you add a short description of what is wrong in the column marked "Issue", and then write the word correctly in the "Correct version" column? The first one is done for you.

Example	Issue	Correct version
healthy	too tight	healthy
h o b b y		
activity		
physical		
fit		
recreation		
walking		
hi ki ng		

Developing your signature

Below are some examples of signature styles.

Signature Signature Signature

Everyone needs to put their signature on various documents. Signatures are used when you are signing important documents, such as work forms, letters and certificates. It is important that your signature be unique and easy to write.

Practise your signature below. Try out a few different versions.

Select your favourite version and keep practising it below, so that it becomes automatic.

Punctuation

Commas are punctuation marks used in writing to separate items in a list or indicate a pause in a sentence.

Copy the sentences below to practise using commas.

Skiing

Skiing is popular in places with snowy climates such as Canada, Switzerland and Italy. There are many types of skiing, including downhill, alpine and cross-country skiing.

Beach volleyball

Beach volleyball is one of the most popular recreational activities in the world. It became an official Olympic sport at the Atlanta 1996 games.

Table tennis

Table tennis, which is similar to ping-pong, is popular in many countries, including China, Vietnam and the Philippines. It is played indoors.

OXFORD UNIVERSITY PRESS

Consolidating

Copy the words in the spaces below and consolidate maintaining consistent slope.

batsman wickets pitch innings

fielding stumps international boundary

Rewrite the following words with the appropriate spacing between the letters.

run out delivery dismissal tournament

Copy the sentences below, and then check the size of your letters.

Cricket is one of Australia's favourite outdoor sports, with matches lasting from a few hours to several days. It is a sport that requires endurance, skill and strategy.

Self-assessment

Use two stars and a wish strategy to write two things about your work you did well, and one thing that could be improved.

Speed test

Write out this word as many times as you can within one minute using print script.

> **Tip!** It is important to master fluency and speedy handwriting. Pracisting your speed in forming letters can help to improve overall proficiency.

achieve

☐ times

Write out this word as many times as you can within one minute using cursive writing. Try to maintain a steady size and spacing as you write.

achieve

☐ times

Write out this word as many times as you can within one minute in capital letters.

ACHIEVE

☐ times

Which way was the quickest? Which was the easiest? Which way was the neatest?

Now we will try the same thing with a sentence. Read the sentence and try to remember it. Write out the sentence as many times as you can within two minutes using fluency joins and speed loops.

Some athletes achieve their dream of representing their country at international competitions.

First try: ☐ words

Second try: ☐ words

Assessment: Fluency and legibility

Copy the text below, focusing on your size, spacing and slope.

Softball is a team sport that involves two opposing teams hitting

a pitched ball and running around a series of bases to reach

home plate. A run is scored when a baserunner safely touches all

three bases and reaches home plate. Each team has nine players,

each of whom gets a turn to bat and to field. Softball is a sport

played by all ages and skill levels

throughout Australia. Softball is similar

to baseball, but the field is smaller,

the ball is bigger and only underhand

pitches are allowed.

Fine motor skills task: Select two of your favourite pictures and sketch them in the box below.

Teacher feedback

Practise your keyboarding skills by typing this passage.